ISBN: 978129036478

Published by:
HardPress Publishing
8345 NW 66TH ST #2561
MIAMI FL 33166-2626

Email: info@hardpress.net
Web: http://www.hardpress.net

THE
SINNER'S COMEDY

John Oliver Hobbes

1/6   .

THE SINNER'S COMEDY

THE SINNER'S COMEDY

BY

JOHN OLIVER HOBBES

AUTHOR OF "SOME EMOTIONS AND A MORAL."

London

T. FISHER UNWIN

PATERNOSTER SQUARE

MDCCCXCII

Photo by Van der Weyde, Regent Stree

JOHN OLIVER HOBBES (MRS. CRAIGIE).

To

ALFRED GOODWIN

(*Formerly Fellow of Balliol College, Oxford, and late Professor of Greek and Latin at University College, London*),

WHO DIED ON

7TH FEBRUARY, 1892.

———

"He was a scholar, and a ripe and good one ;
Exceeding wise. . . .
Lofty and sour to them that lov'd him not ;
But to those men that sought him, sweet as summer."

"Whatsoever he said, all men beleeved him that as he spake, so he thought, and whatsoever he did, that he did it with good intent. His manner was, never to wonder at anything; never to be in haste, and yet never slow; nor to be perplexed, or dejected, or at any time unseemely to laugh; nor to be angry, or suspicious, but ever ready to doe good, and to forgive, and to speake truth : and all this, as one that seemed rather of himselfe to have been straight and right, than ever to have been rectified or redressed. . . .

ANY AUTHOR TO ANY READER

Reader. But where are the Unities?

Author. In life there are no Unities, but three Incomprehensibles : Destiny, Man, and Woman.

THE SINNER'S COMEDY.

————•◦•————

I.

WHEN the ninth Lord Middlehurst lay
on his death-bed, he called each of his
three children to him in turn.   The heir
he bade do his duty, and remember that
Feudalism under a just lord was the
only -Ism for a loyal subject and a
patriot.

The second son he implored to give
up smoking.

The third child, who was his favourite
and a girl, he looked at in silence for a
long time.   When he spoke, it was in a

whisper too low to be heard by the others, who lingered in the room at a distance from the bedside.

"Emily," he said, "all things in life are vanity—save one. That is Love. Find it. It is the philosopher's stone."

He did not speak again till just before he died, when he kissed his wife's hand with singular tenderness and called her "Elizabeth." She had been christened Augusta Frederica ; but then, as the doctors explained, dying men often make these mistakes.

The effect produced on each of the three by the good nobleman's last injunctions was curious and significant.

The heir, who would have been very strong-minded had he been born a woman, had a soul above the management of a country estate. Although all his passions were extremely well-bred and gentlemanly, and had never given him one moment's anxiety from the hour of his birth, there was one—no less gentle-manly, however, than the others—which ruled him with something approaching despotism. This was Ambition. He longed to make a mark, or, to express it more vulgarly, cut a figure. Now, for-tunately or unfortunately, the number of figures which can be cut in the world is practically unlimited ; the only diffi-culty is to cut precisely the kind of figure one would wish. But that merely illustrates the playfulness of the gods. The kind of figure Lord Middlehurst liked to imagine himself cutting was dignified, important, and frock-coated. That is to say, he was to be *the* man on all occasions to wear the Frock-coat and represent in one gracious person the literal and symbolic in Frock - coats throughout cultivated Europe.

He scraped together all his available

capital, raised his rents, and started a Daily Paper.

The Honourable Robert Haviland, who was the second son, was noted for his serenity. When his brother was oppressed with gloom to think how few people he knew who were sufficiently moral to dine with, Robert reminded him that the most interesting sinners usually preferred a supper. His cheerfulness was indiminishable. He shaved regularly for the week following Lord Middlehurst's death, gave his lounging-coat to an under-groom, and began reading religious novels—in bed—as a first step towards reform. At the end of the tenth day he hinted to the coachman that a rat-hunt might be amusing. Before a fortnight had passed, he was limiting himself to four pipes a day—with fluctuating success. " A fellow can't break off a habit all at once," he said ; "it would play the very devil with his nerves, to begin with!"

Emily, who was eighteen at the time of her father's death, married in the following year, at her mother's suggestion, a Mr. Francis Adolphus Prentice, of the firm of Prentice, Rawncliffe, Prentice and Company, bankers, a gentleman of middle age, for whom she cherished the highest respect and esteem. She had met him at six dinners, two tennis-parties, and a court ball. To a young girl marriage only means a trousseau and a honeymoon ; the trousseau she can describe to a flounce : she imagines the honeymoon as a flirtation under the blessing of the Church. Emily, not unmindful of her future husband's brief but destroying small-talk, waived the idea of flirtation, and concentrated her thoughts on the trousseau. Just six

months after the wedding, the unfor-
tunate gentleman died of an illness
which began with a carbuncle and
ended in complications. Emily was
shocked at his death, and grieved
because she could not grieve. He had
been so very kind and so very stupid.
She went in mournful weeds, and
ordered orchids to be placed on his
grave twice a week. Her mother
suggested, " At all events, for the
present."

In stature Mrs. Prentice was rather
above the average height. Her sym-
metry was modern : she was the Venus
of the Luxembourg, not the goddess of
Milo. Her hair, which was fine and
abundant, was of that very light brown
which usually accompanies a sallow
skin. Emily's complexion was like
porcelain, pink and transparent. Her
eyes were blue ; they had the fire and

brilliancy without the coldness of steel.
Her nose and mouth were delicately
formed ; she had a little square chin,
with a cleft which looked like a dimple.
All her features suggested decision and
force : that the decision would be shown
at the right moment, that the force
would be well-directed, was less certain.
" A fine devil spoilt in a saint," said one
man of her. His wife was her dearest
friend—so he had a right to his opinion.

But in the county it was whispered
that Mrs. Prentice was a flirt ; no harm
in her, of course (the " Of Course "
always), yet still—a flirt. A certain estate,
some eight miles away from Hurst Place
(where the lady lived for three months
of the year with her mother), belonged
to a certain baronet, Sir Richard Kilcoursie by name : said Baronet, a
bachelor. Would it be human to suppose that the fair Emily's eyes had not

rolled Kilcoursie-wards ; that, remembering their colour and man's weakness, they had rolled vainly ?   The county— with marriageable daughters—hoped for the best in the case of the Honourable Mrs. Prentice.

Sir Richard Kilcoursie, of St. Simon's Close, in the county of Mertfordshire, started in life as the younger son of a younger son.   Before he was out of his short-clothes, his family decided that he should enter the Civil Service. " Then," said they, " if he only lives to be sixty-three he will have a pension ! " When Richard arrived at years of discretion, he saw no reason for quarrelling with their plan.   Every day of his life brought him nearer the pension, and every day he had the pleasure of spending it in advance.   When Fate made him a baronet, and dropped the hoard of two respectable bachelors into his pocket, he had something like ruin staring him in the face. He never forgot the vision. It sobered his philosophy. He began to take an interest in the workings of Providence. For the rest, he was a man who found no fault with the facts of life so long as they were expressed in picturesque metaphor. The agreeable system of ethics condensed in the axiom that all vices are but exaggerated virtues, seemed to him to breathe a more benevolent spirit than the " *Imitatio Christi.*" He believed that Man was the measure of all things ; that Man was Sir Richard Kilcoursie. His views on Woman were, perhaps, more remarkable for their chivalry than their reverence ; that she lost her youth was a blot on creation : that she could lose her virtue made life worth living. As his nature was sensuous rather than

2

sensual, however, the refinement of his
taste did for him what the fear of God
has hardly done for few.   He waited for
his Eve : she was to be Guinevere, not
Molly Seagrim.   He met her when he
was twenty - three and she nineteen.
Her name was Anna Christian : she
was studying Art in Jasper Street,
Bloomsbury.   At seventeen she had
married an actor—a gentleman with
strong feelings and a limp backbone.
He was an Unspeakable man ; and,
having endured all things, she left him.
It was a bad beginning, but two years'
companionship with the Impossible had
taught her to bear the Necessary with
patience.   She was a woman who
perchance could not have learnt that
lesson in any other school.   "I believe,"
she told her confessor (she was a
Catholic), "I really believe I am almost
meek."   The holy man looked a little

doubtful. "At any rate," she faltered, "I am meeker than I was." He said nothing, but there was a certain eloquence about his eyebrows which appealed so strongly to her sense of humour that she even woke up in the night to smile over it. "I don't care, I *am* meeker," she murmured, and fell asleep again.

Anna was not born, she was made: she had no inherited prejudices, only a consciousness of privilege : she was used to the wilderness, and snuffed up the wind at her pleasure. The men and women she moved among had no philosophy of the artistic temperament : they were its unconscious *data;* they lived, not as they reasoned, but as they felt. And Feeling with them was no psychological problem ; they accepted their moods with their skin as part of the human economy. In their simplicity they were like the philosopher who wrote the whole tragedy of life in the sentence : " *Appetite, with an opinion of attaining, is Hope ; the same, without such opinion, is Despair.*" Anna found in Richard Kilcoursie a man who, though not of her world, showed an immense appreciation for it. If he had no Art, he had at least a Temperament. In his enthusiasm, his impulsiveness, and buoyant sense of irresponsibility, he was like the men of her own people ; he was only unlike them where the difference seemed, in her eyes, immeasurably to his advantage. He had a grace of manner and bearing common enough, it may be, among wellborn Irishmen, but exceedingly rare among the art students, journalists, and actors of Jasper Street, Bloomsbury. Furthermore, he was handsome in the chaste and classic style. In Anna's thoughts he figured chiefly as a Work of Art : that was the first impression he left, and the one which remained when all others were dispelled or forgotten. Richard loved her—or thought so ; she loved him, and thought nothing at all about it. A little close reasoning would have shown her that it was affection and good-fellowship she bore him, and no more. Marriage—even viewed as an impossibility—or the commoner relation in Jasper Street, never occurred to her. Her experience of the married state had been so terrible that she could not trust herself to remember it ; to anticipate even the risk of another such made her pale.

For two years Richard was perfectly happy in her friendship—or, at least, possessed by the excitement which passes so readily for happiness ; for one he was contented ; at the beginning of the fourth year he came into his title. Then life took at once a wider and a narrower meaning : wider, because his interests covered a larger field, narrower, because his own personality—the figure of . Sir Richard Kilcoursie— blocked up the way. Not that his egoism was loud-voiced or swaggering —it was merely constant : if his intellect had possessed an equal stability he would, no doubt, have achieved greatness. As it was, his pleasure-loving mind found satisfaction — if nothing better presented itself — in the unsatisfactory : he endeavoured to elude disappointment with the same persistence as the metaphysician seeks for truth. If his love-bird proved a sparrow, he would discover unimagined charms in the sparrow—not the least of them being that it had been clever enough to deceive him. His companionship with Anna was the one really serious element in his life. Although her attitude towards the world was one of indifference, it was only because she saved her earnestness for her work; she lived for it and, as it were, in it. To be in daily association with a woman so determined and so studious, who, though often mistaken in her opinions, had always the courage of them, gave him a wholesome reverence for those who labour to other ends than cakes and ale. She lived very frugally in two little rooms, and supported herself by illustrating: what time she could spare from that, she devoted to practice in oils. Her Masterpiece, as she called it, was only waiting to be painted: it was all in her mind's eye. The pleasures of her life, outside her work, were few and simple: they mostly consisted in going to the theatre,

when she had orders, and exploring
London.   She and Richard would tramp
for hours through squares and terraces,
crescents, streets and roads—S.E., S.W.,
and W., N., and N.W., and N.E.—
they were never tired till they reached
home, and then there would still be something to talk over, to laugh about and
plan for the next day.   When the
change came in Richard's fortune her
tastes remained the same, but, when
they went to the theatre, they had a box
and a chaperon.   In Jasper Street,
Bloomsbury, where nature was more in
vogue than respectability, a chaperon
was considered an unnecessary and
tedious addition to the ordinary plagues
of life, but Richard explained that
Society which bought pictures was very
different from Society which painted
them : he pointed out, with all possible
delicacy, that although she might not

care for the whims of the polite world,
he, from the habit of his early training,
did and must.

"Do you think, then, you have been
doing wrong all this time?" said Anna,
quietly; "have we sinned in dining together, and talking together, and walking together?"

"Of course not," said Sir Richard,
flushing; "but one has no right to
thrust the details of their private life
and their most sacred convictions. . . .
They wouldn't be understood, to begin
with. People would misunderstand us
altogether."

"What does that matter so long as
we understand ourselves?" said Anna.

"I could not bear to place you in a
false position. I have been far too
careless of appearances as it is. In
that respect I have been abominably
selfish."

The subject dropped : they never returned to it again.   But Society never heard his most sacred convictions.

If Anna had been true to herself, however, at that crisis she would have passed out of his life for ever and begun the world afresh, unfriended.   But while she could face the world, she could not face the loneliness : solitude *à deux* makes solitude only one of two things—perfect rest or complete destruction.   In her case she feared it would mean destruction.   Richard, with all his shortcomings had grown, as it were, part of her nature ; losing him would mean .losing her dearest weakness.   She knew, too, that her influence and affection were more to him than all the moon-swearing passion in the world : that if he could or might love a dozen others for their ears or their eyebrows, or their way of eating bread-and-butter, he would always look to her in trouble and perplexity. She would not desert him. Matters were at this stage when Mrs. Prentice came to Hurst Place on a long visit. Sir Richard then discovered that he was feeling tired of his scheme for happiness. He decided that purity like Anna's appealed to the sentiment of a man, but did not touch his sympathy. Purity itself was too unsympathetic : it had no Past. Anna had a heart, many tender and lovely traits—but she had no passion. He was quite sure she had no passion. It was a pity. Emily Prentice was beautiful ; she was young ; she was witty ; she was a widow—and rich. He fell in love with the Notion of her. About the same time Emily began to wish that he could meet some woman (she was afraid she could not think of *just* the woman) who would lead him into the path of peace. For she had heard rumours of a certain recklessness, of a cynical desperation, of a hey-day philosophy, of a young eagle playing the jackdaw. She felt concerned : she could not sleep for concern. When she happened to meet him on the high-road one morning, she probably blushed for the same reason. He blushed too. Emily said she was quite sure he would be glad to hear that her mother's cold was much better. (The Lady Middlehurst always had a cold when there was nothing more amusing to catch.) He expressed his delight at the tidings. Then, by an odd coincidence, they both began together.

" I think——" said Emily.

" I was wondering——" said Sir Richard.

" I beg your pardon," said she.

" Not at all—I interrupted you."

"I forget what I was going to say."

"So do I."

"Isn't the sky blue?" she said, after a pause; "isn't it beautiful?"

"Very beautiful," said Sir Richard.

"But you are not looking," said Emily, severely.

"I can always see the sky." This was bold. He waited to see the effect.

"Yes, but it isn't always that colour," said Emily, glancing heavenward. For an Angel, it may be, she was a shade subtle.

"Would you be angry if I said something?" said the Mortal.

"How can I tell?" she murmured.

"Do you think I would willingly make you angry?"

"I am sure you wouldn't—willingly. And, in any case, I shouldn't feel anger. I might be hurt, or vexed, or——" she smiled at him with beguiling sweetness, "simply amused."

"It might amuse you, for instance, if I made a fool of myself." Enamoured man is alternately the lover and the turkey-cock.

"Well," said Emily, "after all, you *need* not make a fool of yourself. You are not obliged to amuse me that way, are you?"

"I don't know," he said, impetuously. "I don't know. I only know one thing just at present." He caught her hand. (A country road has its advantages.) "Only one thing, Emily!"

"Oh! . . . That's a stupid thing to know. Forget it!"

"Never."

"Please forget it."

"Never! *never!*"

"But there are other women—much nicer than I am—better worth loving —who would love *you*."

"I don't want any other woman to

love me. I only want to love you.
May I ?"

She looked at him and owned to herself that he was a lover any woman
would be proud of. Honest love, or its
semblance, will always gain a woman's
sympathy even if it fails to win her
heart. To Emily, who doubted whether
she had a heart to lose, it had the added
fascination of mystery. She envied
him his gift of loving. Next to it, she
thought the gift of surrendering were
most to be desired. But she could not
make up her mind to surrender. Free-
dom, too, was not without its sweetness.

"Love is not for me," she said, with
a gentle sigh ; "don't think of it—don't
speak of it. There is nothing in the
world for me but to grow old and die.
That is my future." She sighed once
more and glanced down at her half-

mourning—designed by Worth. "Let us talk of something else."

But his blood was up. The ancestral Paddy (on his mother's side) was tugging at his heart-strings. "Why did God put you in the world—if you are not to be loved and worshipped and—-oh, Emily!"

She laughed in spite of herself. "I am afraid," she said, "God has something else to think of besides my love-affairs!"

"Emily.'

"Yes, Richard." (He hardly liked the *Richard*—it had a sisterly inflection.)

"When may I see you again? Here are those beastly lodge-gates. I must see you soon. Say, to-morrow."

"Well, if you call, you are not to say —the things you have said to-day. . . . In the first place, they are not true."

He saw his opportunity. "*Not* true that I love you; not true that I would

give my life to even kiss your hand"
(which he did on the spot, without
moving an eyelid); "*not* true that you
are the most beautiful——"

"Don't be silly," she said, blushing.

"Do you believe me?"

"I dare say—you think—you are in
earnest." She would not say more.
He, considering it well afterwards, decided that it was enough. He had
some knowledge of the sex.

II.

IN a small studio in Chelsea—a studio
furnished with severe and comfortless
simplicity—a man and a woman were
talking. The man was Sir Richard
Kilcoursie; the woman was Anna Christian. There was something in her bearing which was even majestic; something
in her expression which was childlike
and yet not young—a worldly wisdom
more elfish than mortal. Her pale, deli-
cate face seemed to peep out from the
cloud of black hair which overshadowed
her brows and hung in a large knot at
her neck. A mouth which seemed too
firm to be passionate, and was too pretty
to be austere, grey eyes, full of a tender-

ness which was half mockery, emphasized the contradiction in terms which was the strange characteristic of the whole woman. Sir Richard looked at her furtively, and very often with what was plainly unwilling admiration. He would rather not have admired her that day.

They had been discussing for more than an hour various practical matters relating to his' private affairs : the management of his estate, certain poor cousins, the wages he was going to give his new coachman. Every moment he grew more startled at her intimate knowledge of all that concerned him : he realized, with dismay, that there had been, that there was, nothing too trivial or too deep in his life for her regard.

" There is something you want to tell me," she said, suddenly ; " what is it ? "

He laughed uneasily. " I never can

hide anything from you.   I suppose—
there is—something."

"Tell me then."   Her voice was
singularly rich and well-modulated.

"Do you remember——" he began,
and then stopped.

"Well?"

"Of course you remember that the
Middlehursts are my neighbours.   Did
I ever mention—Mrs. Prentice?   She is
Lady Middlehurst's daughter."

"I don't think you mentioned her,"
she said, drily; "the name doesn't sound
familiar.   *Prentice, Prentice.*   No, you
certainly never told me anything about
an old lady named Prentice."

"I wonder whether you would like
her; but—she's young."

"Young?" said Anna.

"Well, she's twenty-two, or so."

"I was nineteen when you met me!
Is she pretty?"

"In a way, yes. In fact, I suppose—decidedly." He pressed his temples.

"Dark, or fair?"

"Neither one nor the other. There is nothing extreme about her."

"I understand. Tepid! What sort of figure?"

"She is tall and statuesque," said Sir Richard. "I always feel that she ought to have been called Diana. Can you imagine her now?"

The corners of her mouth just curved. "I think I can."

"The fact is—can't you guess?"

"Why should I trouble to make guesses when you are going to tell me *every-thing?*" She fixed her eyes upon his; he could not look away.

"It is hard—in so many words," he stammered.

"You are so like a man! . . . I never thought you were chicken-hearted. You did not seem so when I loved you. Perhaps I should say—when you loved *me*."

" I tell you," he said, springing to his feet, " Emily bores me. Do you think I love her ? Do you think she is like *you ?* " He put his hand with some roughness on her shoulder, and undoubtedly gave her a shake. There was a something in his violence, however, which convinced her far more than his protestations that Emily Prentice very possibly did bore him—or would. Her heart softened.

" You never wanted to call *me* Diana," she sighed.

" I shouldn't dream of her," he said, walking up and down the room—" I shouldn't dream of her if it were not for the estate, and all that. I must have an heir. You see, I really owe it to my people. It's only common decency on my part."

" I thought you did not believe in marriage ? "

" I didn't at one time. I had no responsibilities then—no means. It was very different. A younger son cannot be expected to believe in anything."

" And, is no one expected to believe in a younger son ? " It was seldom she was betrayed into bitterness—a fact which most people attributed to her want of feeling.

" I thought you would make a scene. Women are so unreasonable. I have told you that Emily cannot compare with you. What more can I say ? Even now," he added, a little unsteadily, " I would let my family go to the devil if you would give up your extraordinary ideas and——"

" Richard," she said, gravely, " I will forgive what you were going to say."

" If you cared for me you would not

think you had anything to forgive," he answered, with a harsh laugh. "There is no crime in being Real. But there is so much mawkish, false sentiment about women, that a man is driven to hypocrisy in spite of himself."

"If you want a creature who will love you in your Real moments—if this is one —and in spite of them, you must look for her among the Pollies and Sallies. With them, what they *call* love is the only feeling—they have no others to offend."

Sir Richard looked at her, and wondered. "The truth is," he said, "men can't follow your way of loving. You see, they don't understand it. It's so— so——" he paused for the word—"well, it's so self-possessed."

"When are you going to be married?" she asked, presently.

He felt the awkwardness of the question : Emily had given no promise yet.

" There is nothing definitely arranged —at present."

" Well, I hope you will be happy."

A feeling not wholly unlike disappointment crept over him. For the first time in their history he doubted her love. The thought brought a gnawing loneliness.

" Do you quite understand it all, Anna ? "

" Perfectly. She will be the mother of your heir; you will be faithful to her —in your better moments."

He blushed and said, " You know where to stab."

He could not see her; she touched the back of his coat with the tip of her fingers. That brought her some comfort.

" There is nothing more to be said," he went on.

" Let me see her portrait," said Anna, suddenly.

He pulled a small leather-case out of his breast-pocket.

" How did you know I had it ? " he asked.

" I guessed," she said, with a faint smile ; " you used to carry mine ! " She studied the photograph for some minutes and then returned it. . " You will be very glad," she said, " to remember me."

He looked at her more than half-credulously. She nodded her head. He laughed and went to kiss her. Anna stepped back : her eyes blazed.

" Never do that again," she said.

A china vase—the one ornament in that bare room—stood near the doorway. Sir Richard lifted his cane and struck it. It fell in a dozen pieces.

" You have no heart," he said, " not

an atom. You don't care for me in the least. You never did."

" Yes, I *did*," she answered.

" I will write."

" Yes, write."

" I suppose I must go now."

"Very well." She followed him into the hall. " Richard."

" What ? "

" Say—you don't care a damn ! "

His lips moved, but he uttered no word.

And so he left her.

Her life with Sir Richard had been one of self-abnegation. She had danced to his piping and wept at his mourning : she had been his companion—he had never been hers. At first she had asked nothing better—a peculiarity in woman's love—at first; but, as time went on, the desire to pipe a note or two and mourn just a sigh or so on her own account was often fierce, not to be subdued, a little desperate. Still, he had been kind to her, and faithful according to his lights. She glanced at her easel, but she was in no mood for work that day.· She amused herself looking through an old sketch-book. She found page after page of Richard smoking, Richard sleeping, Richard laughing, Richard scowling, Richard standing, Richard sitting, Richard reading, Richard profile, Richard full-face, Richard three-quarters, Richard back-view. Four of them she rubbed out. She was about to rub out a fifth, when she burst into tears.

III.

Two ladies and two gentlemen were seated in the library of a country-house one afternoon in September. One of the gentlemen wore the gaiters of a Dean. One of the ladies looked as though she would like to wear them, if only for half an hour. As it happened, however, she was dressed in a very tight and evidently very new grey silk, embellished with strings of beads. These jangled and danced with all her movements, to her evident satisfaction and the men's secret despair. She was a small woman and extremely slight, yet, in spite of her slimness, there was not the faintest sign of bone about her ; in fact, it was said that the Dean's sister had not a bone in her body. She was composed of flesh, blood, and spirit.

The other lady, Mrs. Digby Vallence, was tall and spare, with a small face, big eyes, and a large mouth. Digby was fond of saying that his wife's face was geometrically impossible. The parts were greater than the whole. She was a very amiable, intelligent woman, who played Schumann with a weak wrist and was noted for her cookery recipes. Her husband would not have given her for a seraglio of houris.

He himself was a man about fifty, with a clean-shaven face and handsome, clearly-cut features. The ends of his pale yellow necktie were tied with artistic abandon, his short serge coat was of the finest texture, and his loose trousers, of the same material, hung with an idea of drapery about his elegant legs. He.wore the self-satisfied air of the criticised turned critic ; his general expression conveyed that life was one long struggle with his own fastidious-ness—that he practised toleration as the saints did self-denial. Mr. Digby Val-lence was a gentleman of some fame, who had translated Theocritus out of honesty into English, discovered a humourist in Jeremy Taylor, damned Rousseau and, in his leisure, bred canaries. His celebrated paradox, "There is nothing so natural as Art," was perhaps even more famous than he.

"You have never told us," he said, addressing the Dean, "what you think of Mrs. Prentice."

The Dean, who sat in the corner, had a fine, expressive face which suggested his mobile disposition. The type was too unusual to strike a thoughtless ob-

server as anything more than severe ;
women, without exception, called him
odd-looking, and were silent. He did
not appeal to them—to begin with, he
betrayed no desire to appeal to them.
An unpardonable insult. The melan-
choly which clouded his countenance
was neither gentle nor resigned ; on the
contrary, rather fierce and self-mocking.
This fierceness was intensified by a pair
of heavy eyebrows and very piercing
brown eyes. (" One can never lie to
Sacheverell with any degree of comfort,"
said the plaintive Vallence.) He was
tall and well-made, although he stooped
a little and looked some years older than
he really was. In point of fact he was
forty. But a man's age depends on his
history. His history had been dull,
grey, and unromantic—an even saunter
into success which only seemed to him a
crueller name for failure. " Sacheverell

promised to be brilliant," said his college tutor once, " but I am afraid he is only solid. He will be a rock for other men to sharpen their wits on." To guess a man's fate is comparatively easy : to perceive its necessity, its why and wherefore, is given only to the man himself, and then after much seeking and through a mist.

The Dean's sister, Mrs. Molle, was the widow of an Irish major, who had left her his lame hunter, four very healthy little boys, and a dying command that she should do her duty by the children. Sacheverell awoke one morning to find the pitiful group on his doorstep in St. Thomas's-in-the-Lanes, where he held a small living.

" I knew you would be glad to have us," said Eleanor.

The next day his study was referred to as the drawing-room, and he was moved to the attic away from the children's noise.   Eleanor soon complained, however, that the neighbourhood was dull, and the house far too small for comfort.   She had no boudoir, and the nursery chimney smoked.   She gave his old housekeeper notice, and lectured him on his want of ambition.   As a means of advancement she advised that he should get a better living, in a decent neighbourhood; take pupils, and preach Somebody's funeral sermon.   "A man is not supposed to keep a family on a Fellowship," she said.   He glanced guiltily at his violin; it represented half a year's income.

"*That*," said Eleanor, "will lead to nothing but liver-complaint.   Providence sent me to you at the right moment. You do nothing all day but play and dream and scribble.   You surely spend a fortune on music-paper.   I hope you get it at the Stores?"

He shook his head. There was a small shop near—it was so much more convenient ; he could not say what they charged him ; it would be on the bill, no doubt, but when he was in a hurry——

" That is not the sort of thing one is ever likely to want in a hurry," said Eleanor ; " if you send a post-card to the Stores——"

He was, it may be, a little quick-tempered. " I could never order anything—connected with my work—in the same list with soap and Gregory powder and beef-extract. It may be ridiculous, but that is my feeling. Nothing will change it."

But all this happened when Sacheverell was a young man, as the world counts youth, when his dream was to write Masses on Mount Athos. Now he was a Dean, and visited country-houses. " I have made him what he is," Mrs. Molle told her friends; " no wife could have done more for him!"

Men heap together the mistakes of their lives and create a monster which they call Destiny. Some take a mournful joy in contemplating the ugliness of the idol. These are called Stoics. Others build it a temple like Solomon's, and worship the temple. These are called Epicureans. The Dean of Tenchester was a Stoic.

.

" You have never told us," repeated Vallence, "what you think of Mrs. Prentice."

" I suppose," said Sacheverell, " she would be called pretty."

" I have seen her look pretty sometimes," said his sister, at once. " She varies very much. Her hats don't always suit her."

He tried to feel that this was not disturbing.

"Well," said Vallence, leaning back in his chair, with his eyes scanning, as it were, the hidden truths of criticism, "she is not, properly speaking, a pretty woman at all. She is a Manner. To call such a work of exquisite cunning pretty, or even beautiful, is only an attempt at appreciation."

"She is very subtle," said his wife.

"Next time I see her I will look at her more carefully," said Mrs. Molle. She paused, and then asked very suddenly, "Do you think she will ever marry Sir Richard Kilcoursie?"

"She likes Kilcoursie, no doubt," said Vallence. "He is certainly *amour-aché*, and she accepts the situation. I don't suppose he wants her to do more. It is only a very unselfish man who cares to be loved ; the majority prefer to love—it lays them under fewer obligations."

"Do you think they would ever be happy together?" said Sacheverell, slowly.

Vallence shrugged his shoulders. "She must be disappointed in *some* man. To see men as they are not and never could be, is the peculiar privilege of the feminine nature. You see," he went on, "love comes to man through his senses—to woman through her imagination. I might even say, taking the subject on broad lines, that women love men for their virtue ; while men, very often, love women for the absence of it."

"A woman would no doubt need a great deal of imagination to love a man for his virtue," said Carlotta, meekly.

But Vallence was lost in meditation. He had conceived a magazine article to be called "The Pleasing of a Lute," and beginning thus : *The poet in his artificial passion expresses what man feels naturally and needs all his reason to repress.* . . .

" I have heard, as one does hear such things," said Mrs. Molle, "that Sir Richard almost married an actress."

" I think she was an artist," said Carlotta ; " but pray never speak of it before Emily."

The actress who might have been an artist was grateful to Sacheverell's fancy. He had a fine Bohemian instinct. " Indeed," he said, and looked at Vallence.

" Ah," said that gentleman, ever ready to discuss one friend with another—in fact, it was chiefly for this pleasure that he made them—" ah, a curious affair altogether. But it merely illustrates the great law of infidelity in human nature. A man *must* be faithless to something— either to a woman, or his God, or his firmest belief. Kilcoursie certainly appeared very devoted to the other lady—whoever she was. I have heard from several people that they were always together at one time. No one knows her name. They tell me that she looks like Vittoria Colonna."

" Dear me," said Eleanor, thinking that she must hunt Vittoria out in the Classical Dictionary.

Sacheverell strolled to the window. " It has stopped raining," he said. " I think I will go out."

Once in the open air, he threw back his head very much like a dog let loose from his chain. He almost wondered how he had escaped from that close room, the clatter of the tea-cups, the worse clatter of tongues. As a rule, he fell a too ready victim to circumstances : he helped to build the altar for his own sacrifice. To-day, however, he felt rebellious; he was getting tired; Eleanor had disappointed him. When a man gets an idea into his head about a woman, either to her glory or her damnation, whatever she may say or do only gives him one more reason for sticking to it. It is only when he gets an equally strong idea about some other subject, or some other woman, that he becomes nicely critical. Eleanor's virtues had always seemed to him unique; her faults, numerous certainly, were only those of the Universal (preferably, the Homeric) Woman. That afternoon her judgment had been very shallow; she had shown an incapacity to look higher than millinery. It was vexatious. . . .

He remembered his first meeting with Mrs. Prentice. It was the day after his arrival at the Vallences'; she had called in the afternoon on her dear Carlotta: he had told himself he was interested, choosing that word because he knew no other, for no man knows his language till he has lived it. The possibility of feeling more than an ·interest in any woman had never entered his head. He had always kept Passion well within covers on his bookshelf. Emily had talked, with a pretty affectation of learning (feeling, no doubt, that a Dean would look for something of the sort), of Heine, and a new poet, and Palestrina; he had noticed the length of her eyelashes, and her beautiful, unmusicianly hands; hummed, when she had gone, *My love is like a melody*, and reflected, having dined indifferently, that some women were like melodies. The indefinite *"some women"* is an inspiration which comes to every man in his hour of peril. From which it would seem that men and Deans have very much in common. . . . Their second meeting, too, three days later, when she called again, and was pleased to admire his drawings (in the style of Dürer) illustrative of certain passages in Lucretius. He hastened to explain, however, that the philosophy of that poet was unconvincing. "What *is* his philosophy?" said Emily. . . . Then, when he had dined at Hurst Place, how they had disagreed on several points, misunderstood each other with a certain deliberateness, said good-bye coldly. How, the next morning, feeling restless, he had walked on the high-road for no other reason than because it was dusty, unpicturesque, and apparently leading no-whither—suggestive to the Thinking Mind of man's existence ; how *She* had driven past with her mother, bedecked and smiling, disquieting alike to metaphysic and the sober contemplation of telegraph poles. Then at the Tableaux in aid of the New Hospital, when Emily as "Vivien" — under lime-light — had gazed with real sisterly affection on the round and impassive countenance of the Honourable Robert as "Merlin." Sacheverell had felt with some impatience the incompatibility of such trifling with a true appreciation of the seriousness of life ; it showed him that Emily was frivolous, also that her hair fell below her waist. Both discoveries were soul-plaguing : the first because it jarred so horribly, the second because he shared it with assembled Mertfordshire. After the performance he had been the last to come forward : the only one who did not offer some tribute (more or less disguised) to her beauty. " I am afraid," she had said, when she wished him good-night, "*you don't care for Tennyson !* " He made a note in his pocket-book to the following effect : *No man*

*can attain the sublimity of the feminine
egoist.* Frivolity! Egoism! what were
such abstracts weighed against that most
sweet and tangible Feminine. To have
discovered that some woman was Feminine was better than chasing the
Absolute through the Libraries of
Europe. It was, however, but a mo-
mentary rebellion against the ruling
Uncertainty of his life. He had dedi-
cated his days (he lived, from his own
point of view, for two hours every
morning before breakfast, and Eleanor)
to the pursuit of the Absolute. His
work when finished was to be called
" The Metaphysic of Religion " : every
one said it would make him a bishop.
Should he question the glory of the
Unseen because one fair woman was in
sight ? Bitter self-reproach followed his
brief moment of exultation.

" All is vanity," he sighed, at last,

"and discovering it—the greatest vanity." In this frame of mind he looked up, and saw he was near the church. The door was half-open : he heard the organ and recognized the touch. It belonged to no master-hand : it lacked everything that makes a touch—save audacity. He smiled at the childishness of the performance : it was too unaffectedly bad to offend his artistic taste. He pushed open the door and looked in. The player was Emily. She wore a scarlet gown fantastically embroidered in blue and gold ; the light from the flaring gas-jet played on her hair and caught the diamonds on her fingers. In the dark, empty church, she looked to him like some evil spirit risen for his destruction. An evil spirit ! Emily playing " Cujus Animam," with variations.

Sacheverell closed the door softly— she never heard him—and hurried away.

IV.

ALL the tenants of Avenue Villas, Clapham, kept a servant; most of them were on visiting terms. with the curate's wife : here and there one had been known to dine at the Vicarage; one widow, who lived at the corner, had some rich relations who occasionally called on her in a carriage and pair. She was a Baptist, however, and the curate's wife did not even know her name. She fancied it was Grimmage. Mrs. Grimmage, notwithstanding, was a worthy person, and she had a permanent boarder whom the whole of Avenue Villas held in very just esteem. This boarder was a Mr. Cunningham Legge.

By profession Mr. Legge was a humourist : he also wrote the obituaries in *The Argus* (Lord Middlehurst's daily paper) : he devilled for one or two scholarly authors (being great in grammar and punctuation) : he was taster to a poor but eminently respectable firm of publishers : he had written a volume of very graceful Essays himself : " *To the Night - winds and the Moon.*" One critic wrote of them that their style reminded him of Ruskin, the Letters of Cicero and Charles Dickens.

It was generally known that Cunningham was the son of a clergyman, a fact which, apart from his genius and his literary calling, sufficiently explained his poverty ; that his wife had died a few years after their marriage ; that he had never been the same man since ; that he worked from morning till night ; that no one had ever heard him complain.   To look at he was pale, and, to the unseeing eye, insignificant; a man who could sit for hours anywhere and in any company unobserved and silent — indeed, his silence at all times was tragic. To a woman like Mrs. Grimmage it was even awful and mysterious ; she tried to understand him, but could not. He was too dim ; he seemed already in the land of shadows.

His two little girls he kept at a school in the country ; he had no friends who called to see him—if he had any, he saw them in town : the only creature who ventured to Avenue Villas was, oddly enough, a young and beautiful woman. She was his niece, and Mrs. Grimmage knew her as " Mrs. Christian." She had heard Legge address her as " Anna." But she came very seldom, and he never referred to her. Months would pass, when the good Grimmage could only wonder whether she were dead or gone abroad.

"Mr. Legge," she found courage to say to him one day, "is Mrs. Christian a widow?"

"No," he said, quietly.

Mrs. Grimmage had just nursed him through a very sharp attack of bronchitis; she felt she might safely venture on a little light conversation.

"She don't favour you, sir."

"She is my wife's niece."

"Is she anything like her?"

"No," he said; "my wife was beautiful—I cannot tell you how beautiful." For the lover there is only one glory. He paused and sighed; his eyes seemed to pierce into another world.

"Fancy!" said Mrs. Grimmage, "only fancy! Was she very nice?"

"Nice? Dear God! Where did you learn that word? Nice!" He

threw back his head and laughed. But only for a moment. The old dumbness once more took possession of him ; he went silently out of the room and shut himself in his study. Mrs. Grimmage, who peeped in a little later as much from nervousness as curiosity, found him hard at work on his humourous sketch for *The Gossip*.

He had written for more than three hours when he was roused by a sharp tap at the door. He opened it, and Anna, paler and graver than her wont, stood before him.

"Are you busy ? " she said. " Shall I disturb you ? " ·

" I am glad you have come," he said, " I was wondering what had become of you."

She sat down, took off her hat and loosened her cloak. " Now I am here I am afraid you will find me very dull.   I have been working rather hard lately.   I have also been disappointed in one or two things.   Not that I should mind disappointment—now.

Legge glanced at his bookshelves. "Stick to the Immortals," he said, "*they* will never disappoint you.   And they are always there—when you want them."

"Ah," said Anna, "but unfortunately before we can love the Immortals and understand them, we must have some experience of the Mortal."

He sighed, and made no answer.

"Have you any news?" said Anna. "How are the children?"

"They are well.   They write me very happy letters.   Mary has the French prize and Laura has smashed the schoolroom window.   They both want new hats."

"Let me choose them," she said; "they would like them much better if they came from London. Children have a great idea of style." She began to laugh — not hysterically, but without mirth. " Richard is going to be married," she said.

Legge's pale face burned with sympathy. He was not altogether surprised at the news—like most people of melancholic temper, he had a quick insight into human nature. He had known from the commencement, that Kilcoursie's marriage, with some other woman, would be only a question of time. Anna was bearing it better than he had hoped : her lips quivered and she bit them. In that one movement he saw the whole struggle.

" When did you hear it ? " he said, after a long, a painful pause.

"Four days ago. He told me—himself."

" I am afraid it was the only end possible," he said, gently.

" I suppose so."

" Were you — very much — aston-
ished ? "

" A little."

" Will it make a great difference in
your life ? "

" I miss him," she said.   For one
moment her eyes shone—for even tears
have a brief brilliancy, a youth—and
then their light was quenched.   " It is
hard to have no one to talk to.   Do you
think it will take very long to get used
to this—silence ? "

" Not long," said Legge : " you will
be surprised to find how soon—how
very soon you will care for nothing
else."

" He was all—I had in the world," said
Anna, " the one creature who seemed to
love me.   I am not going to cry.   Tears
mean very little.   I have cried.   But
that's nothing."

" Nothing," said Legge, staring into the fire, " nothing."

" This is my birthday," said Anna. " I am twenty-three. I feel very old, much older than you, really, and I—I do feel so tired. I'm afraid I have been overworking."

" Work is good," murmured Legge, " the only good—except Hope. I have lots of Hope."

" Oh, yes," said Anna, " there is Hope." She looked hopeless.

" I have been harder hit than you," said Legge. " I died twelve years ago ; the only thing about me that lives is my stomach. I remember they fed it with chops—on the day *She* was buried. Life is certainly humourous."

They were both laughing when Mrs. Grimmage came in with the tea. She wanted to know whether they preferred scones or muffins.

V.

" You must have loved somebody else once ? "

" Never. In the first place, it is impossible to really love—more than once."

" To *really* love, perhaps—but men have fancies ! "

It was in the music-room at the Vallences'. Emily was taking off her gloves. Sir Richard was watching her. They had both called on Carlotta by appointment to discuss a forthcoming bazaar : Carlotta, with a magnificent instinct, was detained at the Vicarage. The gentle Digby was engaged in his study reviving an old dramatist. He could not be disturbed.

" *Men have died and worms have eaten them,*" said Sir Richard ; " these things will happen."

" Then you *have* had fancies," she said, with just a note of disappointment in her voice (she, too, had a mind for Exceptions)—" was it very long ago ? "

For one brief, too brief moment, he felt tempted to tell her the truth. She was a woman who could hear the truth, and even speak it. It never affected her disagreeably in either case. He thought he might hint something of a youthful madness, and Emily, true to her sex, would no doubt forgive it all with divine generosity, and hate the woman at the bottom of it like the devil.

" I have never had any fancies," he said, at last, and (theoretically) tore up Anna's last note, at that moment in his pocket. But even this did not make her easier to forget.

Emily sighed contentedly. He was reinstated as the Exceptional Man.

" I think that is very nice of you," she said, frankly. " I didn't really, in my heart, believe that you had. I was almost afraid—you are so dreadfully honest—that you were going to confess to—perhaps *one*."

" What do you think of the Dean ? " said Richard, after a pause.

" I don't think he was born to preach to people who want their Heaven to be full of Mansions."

" What do you mean ? "

" Just what I said. It was not a spontaneous criticism. I thought him out this morning when Hawkins was doing my hair. I always reserve that half-hour of the day for sober reflection." She blushed. "I suppose you think I am very frivolous. Women have to be ; no one will take them seriously—not even other women. It is very hard. But what was I saying about the Dean ? Oh— well, there isn't an ounce of Dean about him. He's much too natural."

"What an extraordinary idea ! Don't be angry, but I'm afraid you are not a good judge of character." He coloured as he said it. He had too excellent reasons for 'doubting her discernment. "I never saw any one so stern and un- bending as Sacheverell in my life."

"That sternness is merely self-re- straint," said Emily ; "how much self- restraint do you think the Dean uses to endure Mrs. Molle ? "

"I should say she managed him very well."

"How little men understand each other," said Emily, "how very little. Mrs. Molle is helpless and unhelpful. I shall never forget his expression when Mr. Vallence quoted one day, '*It is better to dwell in a corner of the house-top than with a brawling woman in a wide house.'* And she," added Emily, " she is so unconscious. She thinks she governs him completely."

" How intolerable ! I should hate to think I was being governed. I would do anything for—the woman I loved." (This he said softly, and uttered the word " woman " as though it were some-thing too sacred for his lips—a piece of subtle flattery by no means lost on the sensitive being by his side.) " I would do anything," he repeated, " but it would be knowingly and for love."

" The secret of managing a man," said the Guileless One, " is to let him have his own way in little things. He will change his plan of life when he won't change his bootmaker ! "

" How much you know ! "

" Don't I ? "

He picked up the tassel of her girdle. "That is very pretty," he said ; "those little stones——"

He walked away from her and began to pace the floor. "How long is this to go on ?" he said. "What is the limit to a man's patience ?"

"What do you mean ?" said Emily. "What are you talking about ?"

"I mean—what are we waiting for ?"

"I suppose," said Emily, "we are waiting for Carlotta—and tea." Women have boundless faith in the sobering effect of Commonplace. It is the remedy they administer to disordered passions.

Sir Richard looked at her with something like anger. "This is not a subject which can be changed *that* way. I must speak. I should despise myself if I did not. Do you care—a rap for me ?"

"Yes," said Emily, at once, "I like

you very much. I think you have a
great deal in you. But I want you to
use your talents. I suppose I am am-
bitious for you. A woman likes a man
to be her master. That's a secret. I
want you to be what people say you
could be—if you chose. I hate an
Idler."

" What do you want me to do ? "

" Be of some service to your country.
Be a serious politician."

He could not help smiling. "What !
make speeches and all that sort of
thing ? "

" If necessary—yes."

" Are you in earnest ? "

" In earnest ! " said Emily. " If I
could only tell you a tenth part of all I
would have you do ! But I cannot.
Some thoughts belong to a language we
can't speak." She was wishing that his
eyes were dark and earnest—like Sache-

verell's : that his face had the nobility of Sacheverell's—that he *was* Sacheverell.

" Don't dream about me, Emily," said Sir Richard ; "that sort of ambition is called dreaming. I shall only grieve you when you wake up. I live to amuse myself. I think life is the most lively thing going. I want to enjoy every hour of it. But I must enjoy it my way. And it is such a different way from yours—so very, very different. If you care for me ever so little, let it be for me as I am. I should always be jealous of the Imaginary Me. I would know I was only his shadow."

" I do—like you as you are," murmured Emily. " I am sure I am not mistaken."

" Do you like me well enough to be my wife ? "

" I don't know—I —you see—I—don't

want to be anybody's wife — just yet."

" I will wait—I will wait as long as you wish. I only want to know that some day——"

Some day sounded a lifetime distant. " Who knows—what might happen— some day ?" she said.

He drew a long breath. " Will you promise ?"

To promise that something would happen some day seemed even childish in its simplicity. " If you like," she said, half-laughing.

" My love for you," he said, " is a power outside myself. I cannot control it—*it* controls me. It is for you to decide whether for good or evil." Dimly it occurred to him that he had said something of the kind once before—to Anna. " I will try to be worthy of you," he added. She was a very pretty woman. He stooped and kissed her hand.

Just then Sacheverell entered the room.

"They told me you were here," he said; "I have come to say good-bye. I have just received a telegram which calls me back to town. I must catch the 5.40."

He looked so unlike himself that Emily faltered, "I hope it is not bad news?"

"A very old friend is dying," he said; "he has sent for me. That is all."

"I am sorry," said Emily.

"If he lived it would be sadder."

"How is that?" said Sir Richard, who was admiring Emily's mouth.

"Because," said Sacheverell, sternly, "his life has been all work and suffering."

"I am sorry," murmured Emily again.

"Do not pity him. He has chosen

6

the good part. Good-bye." He shook
hands with them both and went out.

" He is very depressing," said Sir
Richard, after a pause. Emily did not
hear. She was listening to the echo of
Sacheverell's footsteps as it grew fainter
and finally ceased.

" I believe you rather like him," said
Sir Richard, jealously.

" He was interesting. He has made
me forget three headaches !"

" Yes ? A man may give his whole
life to a woman, and it won't mean so
much to her as if he had once jawed her
out of neuralgia !"

" And a woman," said Emily, " may
give her soul for a man, and he won't
think so much of her as if—she had
jilted him for somebody else."

Sir Richard laughed. "We must not
take human nature too seriously ! That
is the mistake which lies at the root of

all the misery and discontent in the world !"

Then Carlotta came in—apologetic but smiling.

VI.

" WHAT is the time, Anna ? "

"It is past eleven, uncle. He will not come now. You must wait till morning. Besides, there is no hurry. Won't you try and go to sleep ? "

" He said he would come, and he will be here. He always keeps his word. Put the clock where I can see it, dear, and go to bed. If I want anything, I will ring."

" I am not tired enough—to go to bed," said Anna, whose eyes were heavy with watching. " Let me read you to sleep. If Dean Sacheverell comes, I can wake you."

Legge had been ill for nearly a fortnight. They said he had not rested sufficiently after his attack of bronchitis; he had tried his strength too soon : they called his condition a relapse. He knew it was the end, because he felt so happy. " To see you lying in bed and not fretting and grizzling over it, is a perfeck treat ! " said Mrs. Grimmage.

" I have no book to finish this time," he said, smiling ; " *that* is all done."

When he told them—for Anna, too, had come to nurse him—that he wished to see a friend, it was regarded as a hopeful sign. There was a touch of the Usual and Human in the desire which cheered the soul of Sarah Grimmage. " He only wants livening up, bless you ! " she said to the doctor.

Anna fell asleep in her chair while Legge watched the clock. At a quarter to twelve Sacheverell arrived,

" I suppose," he said, "you had given me up ? "

" No," said Legge, " " I knew you would come."

Sacheverell just noticed that a pale woman with grey eyes murmured something to the sick man, and left the room. In some way she seemed a remarkable woman—quite unlike any other woman he had ever seen. As he looked at her, it seemed like reading an unfinished tragedy—with the catastrophe to be written. When she had gone, Legge turned to him and sighed.

" That is my Dearest's niece," he said, " the one whose mother—had a history —you remember. I should feel so glad —if it were not for her. I am not much to her, but when I am gone she will have no one. She has had a terrible life. I wanted to tell you some of it—I am afraid I'm hardly strong enough—tonight." He spoke with great difficulty, and between long pauses. "A brave woman—and good. Strange—you were stopping—with the Vallences. Never mention—Kilcoursie—if you met him. I don't seem able—to say much—now you have come . . . a lot of things— good of you to come. I shall not forget . . . . I knew you would. The children——." He closed his eyes, but said presently : "I have been waiting to see my Dearest—so long. She will think I have changed." A faint smile moved his lips. "I am rather sleepy. You don't mind ? "

Sacheverell sat down by his side and waited.

Mrs. Grimmage and Anna, in the meantime, were talking with some show of blithesomeness in the next room.

"If you want to know my idea of a Man," said Mrs. Grimmage, "the Dean is my idea to the very life. The moment I clapped eyes on him, I said to myself, ' That is a Man,'—and meant it. I suppose he's married. He's got a sort of patient, bearing-up look. Perhaps she's a currick's daughter, and a fright. Men are wonderful poor judges of looks. They will pick out girls that you and I wouldn't look at a second time, and go raving cracked after 'em. I know 'em. You can't tell me anything about Men. But I like a man to be manly. Let him be decent, I say, but let him be a Man." She looked wise over this dark utterance.

" A man's way of loving is so different from a woman's," sighed Anna.

" There ain't nothing," said Mrs. Grimmage, " there ain't nothing that makes them so sulky and turns them against you so soon as saying anything like that. And that's a mistake girls always make. They begin the heavenly.

It's not a bit of use being heavenly with men. Just you remember that. You must take 'em as they are, or leave 'em."

" I see," said Anna.

" There's many a young woman lost a man's love," observed Mrs. Grimmage, " by coming the heavenly."

" She's better without it," said Anna, " much better."

" The most faithfullest man I ever see," said Mrs. Grimmage," is your poor dear uncle. But then he's eccentrick— ain't he ? And he ain't the sort as many 'ud fancy for a sweetheart. He ain't dash-ey enough. Women do like a bit of Dash. I do myself."

At that moment Sacheverell tapped at the door. The room adjoined Legge's.

" It is over," he said, gently.

Mrs. Grimmage uttered a cry. " Oh, sir, what do you mean ? Whatever do you mean ? "

Anna put her hand to her heart. She followed Sacheverell to the bed where Legge was at rest.

" How happy he looks," she said.

" I never know'd he was so handsome," sobbed Mrs. Grimmage.

He had the face his wife knew, and was young again.

The settlement of poor Legge's affairs proved a very small matter. Beyond his few books and pictures and a little plain furniture he had nothing in the world. He had always spent his money as he earned it : sometimes he could have spent rather more than he earned, and still lacked much which many men would have considered necessary to existence. His two little girls, whom he kept at a happier and more cheerful home in the country than he could give them in his lodgings, had all his income save the

two pounds a week he kept—unwillingly
—for his own use. He never allowed
himself to think how he longed for his
children and the brightness they might
have brought into his life. He only
thought of what was best for them.
They were left totally unprovided for :
the sale of his effects produced, as
Sacheverell told Anna, two hundred
pounds. As` he was the purchaser, he
probably knew. Lord Middlehurst, out
of consideration for his services to *The
Argus*, paid his funeral expenses and the
doctor's bill : he also gave him a short
obituary, in which he referred very
handsomely to his brilliant talent and
excessive modesty, " *which alone kept
him from that high place in the public
regard which,*" etc., etc., etc.

" I will take care of the children," said
Anna.

" You ?" said Sacheverell. She seemed

so very young for the burden.   But she
smiled.

"I am getting on pretty well, you
know," she said.   " I am more fortunate
in my publishers than my poor uncle.   I
—I draw a little."

Her white face—her slight form—it
was all so childish and pathetic.   " The
artistic profession is the hardest in the
world for a woman—in fact, any artistic
profession is hard for anybody," he said.
" Art means labour—hard, ceaseless, un-
satisfying labour.   Her service is work,
and her reward—the strength for more
work."

" I have drawn ever since I can remember," said Anna ; " it came to me
like speaking.   When I was old enough
I studied hard.   I made up my mind
that painting was to be my work in life.
*'Tis no sin, you know, to follow one's
vocation.*   They called me a fool, and

they said I would starve. I did starve for a time. I could wish I had starved a little longer. But I married. I forgot my work." She coloured. " I soon remembered it again. I decided to study quietly by myself for a year or two—any number of years, for that matter—I did not care how many, so long as I could see Hope at the end. I was working when—when I came to nurse my uncle. I think I must win—perhaps not yet, but some day. Every failure will only make me stronger when I succeed. I am so hard to discourage! Pain and despair and heartache—they cast you down for a while, but afterwards—they help you to understand." It did not seem at all strange then that she talked to him so openly, but it was very wonderful to remember in later days.

Sacheverell listened with almost painful interest. Her story with its suggestion of a tragedy in little was sad enough : what he feared was her mistaken confidence in her own ability seemed to him even sadder.   Genius is so rare, and ambition is so common.

" I should like to see some of your work," he said, at last.

" If you can call at my studio to-morrow," said Anna, laughing, " I will show you my Masterpiece ! "

He did not go immediately, however, but stayed an hour longer.   They sat in the window of Mrs. Grimmage's draw-ing-room, and talked very happily, if inconsequently, on many subjects, from Browning and Bach to Mazzini and Plato.   They were very cultured, indeed.

" Did you see that woman who passed just now ? " said Anna, suddenly.

" Yes."

" She had beautiful hair — Venetian red.

"I saw it."

She looked at him with something like gratitude. The artistic sympathy is very subtle — terribly irresistible. "How lovely," she said, "to be with somebody who *does* see things. I could tell you the whole history of that woman," she went on, "just from her walk. She does not care for that tramp—he doesn't understand her—he doesn't even know that her hair is magnificent. But she wants to Belong to somebody."

"When a man suspects that his God is not taking him seriously, he changes his religion," said Sacheverell; "are women less philosophical?"

"Gods are so scarce," sighed Anna; "if a woman finds even a false one—she thinks herself fortunate."

For the next twenty minutes they played at disagreeing. Such flat disagreement was never heard within those peaceful walls. "I shall have more to say on the subject to-morrow," said Sacheverell, when he left.

"I could say miles at this minute," said Anna.

After he had gone she drew him, from memory. The result was such a miserable failure in her eyes that she burnt it—with a refinement of cruelty—by inches. Nor did she ever attempt to draw him again. It may be that a suggestion, a hint of him, cropped out occasionally in the turn of a head, in an arm, or in a look round the brows, but that was all. She kept the Man to herself : he could not be chopped into illustrations.

Sacheverell had guessed from Legge's remark that Anna was none other than the mysterious artist who looked like Vittoria Colonna. It was strange that he should have met her—very strange.

Having met her, he was quite certain that the love had been all on Sir Richard's side : that the story was all on Sir Richard's side. That such a woman could care for such a man was impossible. It was easy to understand, however, why Mrs. Prentice might care for him. He had given very little thought to Emily since the evening she had played in the church. He remembered her as one remembers some certain night in June—that it was perfect for June—that a year of such would be unhealthy. He had mistaken *la grande passion* for passion. It consoled him to call to mind that Marcus Aurelius had also fallen into some fits of love, " but, was soon cured." Emily's face came upon him—it was less lovely than Anna's, more bewitching, more human, less spiritual. He thought he had read her character very truly at first sight. She

7

was Circe. Reconsidering his decision however, at a distance of four weeks and sixty miles, he saw that there were weak points in the Circe theory. Emily was the Popian—merely Popian—coquette : perhaps too fond of admiration : decidedly weak. Pretty? yes, if one admired the opal—set in brilliants. Her hair always smelt of violets. (Scent got into one's brains.) There was none of that mincing sensuality about Anna.

When he saw her at her studio the next day, she was very quiet and grave. The only canvas in the room had its face to the wall.

" I am very nervous about showing it to you," she said; " no one else has seen it. I am so afraid you will think it is rubbish. If you do," she added, " I shall cut it up—and start afresh."

" Even if I think," he said, awkwardly, " that you have hardly had experience enough yet — you see, you are very young————"

He felt he could never flatter her— never pay her mere formal compliments. If her work were bad, he would have to say so.

She went slowly towards the canvas. He was anxious himself, and could not understand the anxiety. It was a new sensation. He ·dreaded to see her failure ; the suspense was intolerable.

" Is the light good ? " he began.

" Excellent," said Anna. Neither of them knew what they were saying. " There," she said, placing the picture on the easel. " The subject is ' The Flight of Pompilia.' " She quoted Browning's lines very softly—half-un-consciously :—

> " Between midnight and morn
>
> .   ·   .   ·   .   ·
>
> Began a whiteness in the distance, waxed
> Whiter and whiter, near grew and more near,

Till it was she: there did Pompilia come:
The white I saw shine through her was her soul's,
Certainly, for the body was one black
Black from head down to foot."

"You were right to work," he said, at last.

"Shall I go on—working?"

"By all means."

"That is all I want to know," said Anna.

"There are many things I should like to say," said Sacheverell. "You have great power. . . . You know what I think—what I *must* think."

She blushed and smiled.

"I have worked very hard," she said. "If you could see the yards of canvas I have burnt! I have been painting and burning ever since I was six. . . . So you like it? Of course, it is not quite finished. I work very slowly. Lately I have accomplished so little—so very little. The illustrations take all my time, and when they are done I am too tired to paint."

" Then why don't you give up the illustrating ? "

She smiled at him sadly. " I must keep body and soul together, and—I have some one dependent on me." This was the first reference she had ever made to her husband. Sacheverell felt at once, by a sort of intuition, that the some one else was the always-absent, always-present Christian. " I made one great mistake in my life," she said, gravely. " Some day I may tell you about it." Then they talked of other things.

" I know—about your book," said Anna, at last ; " my uncle told me. Why won't you finish it ? "

" That is nothing in the world," he said, briefly. " Why did Legge tell you ?'

" One day, when he was ill, I went to his desk—I was the only one he allowed to touch his papers—and I found a manuscript. I was unhappy at the time, but I read it, and somehow, my despair went away. I felt I might yet do something with my life. I asked who wrote it. Then he told me it was yours, that it belonged to your book, and how you put it aside when your sister—when you became a rector—somewhere."

" You see," he said, with an attempt at a laugh, " I, too, have some one dependent on me, and I—like you—work slowly. Still, as a matter of fact I write now, when I feel in the mood. I have a certain amount of leisure. Just now I am supposed to be resting. I have had rather a hard year, but next year may not bring so much care, and then——"

" But—you are not happy," she said.

"Perhaps not. I don't think that matters. I will finish my work some day. I shall finish it for you."

"Promise me," said Anna.

"I promise."

She held out her hand to say good-bye.

"Not that hand," he said, "the other. You give your right hand to every one."

The extraordinary thing was that this did not seem extraordinary to either of them. They had seen a great deal of each other—though the length of their friendship could be reckoned by days.

VII.

THAT night, Sacheverell received a letter from his sister.

"MY DEAR PETER," it ran—"As it is so much more agreeable here than it is in town or at home just at present, Carlotta *insists* on my remaining another fortnight. I think this is a splendid opportunity to have the dining-room whitewashed and the drawing-room papered. The paint in my bedroom, too, would be none the worse for a fresh coat. As you are in town, perhaps you had better go straight on to Tenchester and remain there to look after the workmen. They need *incessant* watching. Get somebody to inspect the drains. I am so dreadfully afraid of typhoid—one hears such awful things—and now Frank is coming home I want to be *quite* sure that the house is healthy. I have been thinking that *you* might as well move into the back bed-room and let him have yours. There is such a nice wall there to hang his trophies on. We shall never get them all into the drawing-room. Would you like the smaller lion's skin for your study? It is so dark there that no one will be able to see that it is torn.

" Mrs. Prentice is flirting desperately with Sir Richard. She will, no doubt, marry him. They are pretty certain to ask us to St. Simon's-in-the-Close. She and I have seen a great deal of each other lately. All the Havilands are useful people to know. Lord Middle-hurst has a *tremendous* lot of influence. He might do something for one of the

boys.   I want Lionel to get a secretary-
ship; he has his father's charm of
manner.   Darling Percy!   But it does
not do to think of him.   Bye the bye,
don't forget to have all the lamps
thoroughly overhauled.

"Can you make up a parcel of your
old clothes (*under*-things, of course)
and send them to me here?   I have
promised them to the under-gardener.
He is so grateful to me, poor creature.   I am sure the little change down
here did you good.   You don't rest
sufficiently.   I *cannot* get you to be
idle.   Why you should take all this
trouble about that extraordinary Cunningham Legge I cannot imagine.   Such
waste of time, too, for a man with your
responsibilities.   Your friends (particu-
larly the *nobodies* and those who have
nothing on earth to do) seem to think that
you have nothing to do but to fetch and

carry for them. I wonder why you put up with it. *I* wouldn't for one moment.

"I don't wish to worry you, but I think you ought to stir yourself about 'The Metaphysic of Religion.' By the time you have finished it all your ideas will be old-fashioned. You don't seem to have any ambition. I am quite sick of telling people that you hope to publish it soon. I am sure they think it will end like that tiresome old Casaubon's 'Key to all the Mythologies.' Mr. Vallence hinted something of the sort at lunch to-day. Why do you trouble with all these committee meetings and things? *Other* Deans don't do it. I was trying to remember yesterday how many people you buried last year. I really think you might drop the burying. It means a whole afternoon every time. When do those awful Divinity students begin work? It seems to me you take far too great pains with *them.* They are not worth it. Still, as they pay very well, you can't give them up just at present.

" If Lord Middlehurst puts Lionel up for the *Junior Devonshire*, the entrance fee won't be *more* than fifty. I forget the *exact* amount—but it will be such a good thing for him. In one way it is rather an awkward expense just now. I was rather hoping that you and I could manage a little run to Bellagio later on. I need a rest fully as much as you do. There's the dinner-gong.

" Your affectionate sister.

" E. MOLLE.

" P.S.—I want some money for a few bills. Better send a blank cheque."

He read this through and laughed : it reminded him of so many others in the same strain. At one time it would have filled him with bitterness, but now

—could he not see Anna on the morrow ?
He sat down to write : he had a few
ideas. This was the first :—*Thoughts,*
when the mind is thrall to some strong
emotion, come in a sort of rhythm: it
may be said that we think in a rough
kind of blank verse. He paused, then
wrote rapidly on another slip of paper :

> She seemed a flower—heiress to all the beauty,
> All the grace and fragrance of each flower
> Sprung since the world began.

He read it critically — frowned —
smiled. It was, at least, spontaneous ;
he could grant that. He read it again
—*She seemed.* Ah ! why had the word
seem occurred to him ? There was an
example of the mind unconsciously
hedging. He wanted the Truth, not
the Semblance. It might be that the
Real Anna was plain - featured and
ordinary : a little, dumpish woman :

sallow, somewhat shrewish. Oh, that a man's eyes should be such traitors to his Perception! He remembered that he had suffered the same harassing doubts in the case of Mrs. Prentice. "*Adgnosco veteris vestigia flammæ*," he murmured, and passed a sleepless night.

On the morrow, when he called at the Studio he made no excuse for his visit. He went as a matter of course : it seemed, indeed, the only thing to do.

As for Anna—she expected him, and wore a useless but adorable silk pinafore. The colour was pink : it pleased him to call it rose-jacynth. He decided, for all time, that she was lovely. And he was not mistaken.

VIII.

AFTER Sacheverell had left the Vallences', Emily's whole manner changed. Her gaiety was astonishing. To Carlotta's dispassionate mind it seemed rather hysterical : her laugh was so much merrier than her eyes : her wit had the saltness of tears. Carlotta could not think she was unhappy. Every circumstance forbade the suspicion. As for Emily herself, she tried to believe—and to a certain extent succeeded in believing—that she was supremely contented. To be pretty, to be rich, to have a devoted lover—could she ask for more ? To Go as much as one could, and Think as little as one might, was the secret of happiness.

"Thought should be unconscious," said Sir Richard; "it is a natural process like digestion."

"Perhaps you are right," sighed Emily.

She was too impressionable, too quick with her sympathy and too imaginative to be rigidly faithful to any one creed or any one creature. She could weave fairy garments for the ugliest scarecrow: if Ferdinand were absent she would find something to adore in the present Caliban. Was Sacheverell right, she wondered, was Work and Suffering the good part; or was Sir Richard—with his laws of Nature, and that Nature a smiling goddess—right?

"At one time," said Carlotta to her one day, "I thought you liked the Dean. He has not such charming manners as Sir Richard, but one can hardly compare them."

" *Hyperion to a Satyr*," said Emily.

" What ! " Carlotta's eyes opened wide.

" I—I did not mean Sir Richard by *Hyperion*."

" Emily, I'm afraid you are fickle."

" Perhaps I am."

" But if you liked the Dean——"

" I didn't exactly *like* him. I might have, but——you see, I know quite well he despises me."

" How could he ? "

Emily remembered the last look he gave her. " Well, I suppose he is more sorry for me than anything. It was so unpleasant, you know—he happened to come into the music-room when that stupid Richard was kissing my hand. I couldn't explain that it really wasn't my fault. I don't suppose I shall ever see him again. I don't care a bit—only—it isn't nice to know that

8

he has got *quite* a wrong impression of me."

"One of these days," said Carlotta, "your flirting will bring you unhappiness. Sir Richard is not a man who will stand nonsense."

"Don't frighten me," said Emily, who was trembling already. Carlotta's words only confirmed her own fear.

"Do you love him?" said Carlotta.

"I don't know," said Emily. "I suppose I do—in a way. I am afraid of him. He is so determined."

"I wish you had never met him!" said Carlotta, prime instigator of their meetings.

"So do I," said Emily, with a sort of whimper.

"Have you promised to marry him?"

"He thinks I have. It comes to the same thing. Oh dear!"

"My dear Emily, this is too ridiculous."

" It's dreadful. But what can I do ?
I was never so worried in my life. We
are going to Egypt. Egypt is *newer*
than Paris. And a quiet wedding —just
in my going-away dress. Do you think
that a pale shade of grey trimmed with
sable tails——"

" Why can't you be honest and admit
that you are in love with him ? "

" Well, he *is* very nice. You should
hear him read Herrick. He feels every
word of it, and it is not as though he
were a man who had been in love a
hundred times. I am the only one.
Just think—out of all the women he has
met. We *must* be happy."

" You can't command the Future,"
said Carlotta, stonily.

" Let me think I can," said Emily,
" that's half the battle," and (she was
spending a few days with Carlotta)
she went out of the room singing.

Nevertheless when she found herself in her own bedroom, with the door locked, she cried. She herself could have given no cause for her tears : that was the worst of it. It was an unsatisfactory misery in every sense — without beginning, or middle, or end, or reason, or hope. She paused once in her weeping to wonder what she could wear down to dinner. There was the velvet with *point de Flandres.* Sacheverell hated velvet, but Sacheverell was not there to see. The sobbing continued. To be loved was better than loving—much better. She would marry Sir Richard, who *worshipped* her, and forget—— There was no one to forget.

At dinner that evening she was dazzling. Sir Richard was there.

In the drawing-room, afterwards, Mrs. Molle and Carlotta sat by the fireplace and discussed bronchitis. Digby was

confined to his room with neuralgia—
and an adverse criticism. Sir Richard
saw his chance. There was a window-
seat some distance from the fire. Would
Emily sit there and watch the stars? He
knew a little about astronomy.

" This is our last night here— for some
time," he said, in a low voice. " It is
never so nice at Hurst Place."

" This is certainly very pleasant," said
Emily, "What is the name of that star?"

" Do you remember what you
promised ? "

" I have promised ever so many
things, haven't I ? I hope I shall be
able to keep some of them."

" You *must* keep *one.*"

" That wasn't a promise—exactly.
And I forget. What was it about ?"

" You do not forget."

" Do take care ! They will see you.
You are hurting my hand. I suppose

I *do* remember. How you tease! Besides—I was in fun."

" I was not."

" Well, what do you want me to do ? "

" I want you to marry me."

"Marriage is so dull, Richard. There would be no more Herrick. . . . We are so happy as we are. Why spoil it ? Men are never satisfied!"

" Yes, they are. If it were not for that Molle person and Carlotta! Shall we ever be alone together—ever able to talk except five yards apart, with our eyes on the door or some old woman ? I am sick of it. This is the sort of thing that drives people into matrimony. Don't laugh at me—it *is*. Emily, meet me in town on Monday. Let us be married quietly — by special license. We won't tell any one about it. You need only regard it as a form of engagement—if you like. I only want to know that you belong to me—that whatever happens, you are my wife. Is that much to ask—when I love you as I do?"

"Wouldn't it seem odd? What would people say?" The idea, however, appealed to her. Though it spelt a marriage certificate, it sounded like throwing her cap over the wind-mill. Irresistible witchcraft! Her eyes sparkled.

"What fun!" she said.

Everything, he saw, depended on his self-restraint. A movement, an expression, a word too much or too little, and his case would be ruined. That she was a nice problem in diplomatics was not the least considerable of her fascinations: he could never be sure of her. She was not a woman one could woo dozing. He looked round. Mrs. Molle and Carlotta had gone into the little boudoir which led off from the drawing-room. He could hear their voices : they were searching for a mislaid letter. Swiftly and boldly he caught Emily in his arms and—did not kiss her. He just put his lips to her ear and said, "You are so beautiful!" Badly managed, the thing would have been a hug. Unspeakable vulgarity! As he did it, however, it was a movement of much grace indicative of passion.

Emily said nothing.

"Dearest, you will come on Monday?"

She lifted up her face to say "No." It somehow got mixed on the way with a "Yes" from Sir Richard. The combination was no syllable.

They were married, however, by a Bishop, assisted by an Archdeacon. Every one agreed that it was even grander than her first wedding.

IX.

FOR Sacheverell the sun had not set for a fortnight : for Anna, there had been magic in the moon. They had seen each other every day : they had been for several strolls into the country. She always walked with him to his hotel or till they were in sight of it, and he invariably walked back with her again to her studio. The childishness of the performance caused them endless merriment. They also read together : once or twice they managed to finish a whole paragraph. For some reason, however, she never touched her picture. " I can always paint," she said ; '' I have been painting all my life. I have not always

had you—nor can I have you always."
He had told her that he loved her;
she had made answer that men were
very fickle : that Love was the Eternal
Lie, and the man who told it the prettiest
was the best poet. She, herself, was
not, as the phrase goes, in love with him,
but she was under his influence. Sacheverell's dreamy, speculative mind was
especially delightful to her, a woman
who had never found leisure for dreaming, and to whom the high sphere of
speculative thought was an undiscovered
country. There was a gentleness, too,
in his character, a resignation to the will
of God—or of anybody—which seemed
divinely meek to her more rebellious
nature. When she told him the long
story of her short life, of her husband,
of Kilcoursie, she forgot all her past
unhappiness in the fact that he, in the
Present, was listening and understanding.

" Talking to you," she said to him, " is only thinking to myself—made easier."

That evening he was to meet Mrs. Molle at Paddington, whence they would leave for Tenchester. He could not see Anna for at least ten days.

" It will be strange to-morrow and to-morrow," she said, " not to have you with me."

"And I——" said Sacheverell.

"Will you miss me ? "

"You know I will."

" I am so glad. . . . I ought not—it's hateful—but I want you—to be miserable." She opened a cardboard box which stood in a corner of the room, and produced an unconsidered trifle in the shape of some ribbons and feathers. She put it on her head, and in so doing managed to brush some tears from her eyelashes.

" Do you like my new hat ? " she said.

This was her way of changing the subject.

" Is that bow meant to stick up ? "

" Of course ; flat bows are hideous.
Nothing would induce me to alter it.
Nothing. . . . Perhaps you will like it
better .when you get used to it."

" Perhaps."

" *Why* don't you like it now ? "

" I do," he said.

She smiled with happiness. " I love
nice clothes. I could live in a garret
and sleep on the floor and eat bread and
apples, or bread without the apples—but
I *must* have pretty gowns."

" You are very beautiful in anything," he said.

" If you think so," she answered, as
gravely, " it will make me beautiful."

" Anna," he said, quickly, " if we
could be together always ! "

" Together—always," she repeated.

"Just think of it—you with your painting and me—who knows? I might finish my book. We might go to Mount Athos."

"On Mount Athos," said Anna, "there would be no philosophy—but a fiddle and some picturesque rags."

" I am afraid we must not drop philosophy," he said.

" In that case," said Anna, " we must drop Mount Athos and take an attic. It would have to be an attic—we should be so poor. But we would work and work and work. Between us we might accomplish something ! Would the days ever be long enough ? I would do the cooking. I can make an omelette and a beef-steak pie—but I have forgotten most of the pie. Do you mind ? "

He laughed. " Should we be able to afford beef-steak ? "

" We should be called The Dean and
his minx," said Anna. " *What* would
Eleanor say ? "

" Suppose we went down and resigned
the Deanery together," he suggested.
" But are you—crying ? "

" No, it is only the light—it is a little
strong for my eyes. I—I have been
using them too much lately. Ten
whole days to wait—before I can see
you again. It seems such a long time.
So many things can happen in ten days.
. . . I will work at the picture, but—
sometimes I think it will never be
finished. Whenever I see hope something happens. I—I heard to-day,"
she went on, " from my husband. He
is in money difficulties again. The
thirty pounds I sent him to pay some
bills with he has used for something
else. So he wants another thirty.
That means I must accept Stock's offer

for the black and whites. I am getting so tired—and worried. I am strong really—very strong. I *ought* to be able to work nine hours a day—but I can't."

" And I can do nothing to help you ? " said Sacheverell. " Must I see you toiling like this for that man ? Am I powerless ? a log ? a stone ? "

" I shall be all right," she said, " if you write to me every day. You have given me so much courage that nothing seems too hard for me."

Their farewell was in silence.

Her letters for the next week were full of humour—of hope—of plans for the future. "Seventy-two more hours and then I shall see you. I am so glad, that I feel almost afraid to think of it." So she wrote in the morning. That same night she sent another note to say she had received word that her husband was lying seriously ill—at the point of death—alone in his lodgings. "I must go to him," she wound up. "I will do what I can. He has no friend in the world. The very sight of him stifles me. I would sooner house with a rattlesnake than go near him. But he is ill. I have no choice in the matter."

Sacheverell, who knew the horrors of her married life as no one else knew them, read her letter and felt it was her death warrant. He was staring at it when Eleanor rushed into the study waving the *Pall Mall Gazette.*

"The Bishop of Gaunt is dead," she panted, and looked the rest. He neither heard nor saw her.

"George is not so ill as I expected," Anna next wrote; "he is certainly weak, but there is nothing really serious the matter with him. I cannot help thinking—well, perhaps you can guess. Still, as I am here, I will not leave him till he is convalescent. I am not feeling very well. My eyes pain me. I am obliged to work at night when he is asleep. Of course, it is a strain. I hope to be out of the house on Saturday." The note was dated Thursday. On Sunday morning Sacheverell received the following :—

"14, CARBURY STREET,
TOTTENHAM COURT ROAD.

"DEAR SIR,—My wife desires me to say that she has been unable to finish the drawings she promised you. She is not well enough to write herself, but she hopes to be able to do so in a few days.

"Yours very truly,
"GEORGE CHRISTIAN."

9

During the four months that followed —months of such dull madness that it seemed sanity—Sacheverell managed to hear both directly and indirectly how she was. Not that inquiries were necessary—he knew by a strange instinct, her good days and her bad days. He also knew that she would never recover.

" At one time you thought you would like to be a Bishop," said Eleanor ; " now you have got your wish you don't seem to care a bit."

" I believe I am called a Bishop," he answered, with a strange smile. " Poor Doddridge ! "

Doddridge was his predecessor.

X.

ANNA wrote to him at last to come and
see her.

The day was dim : rain seemed to be
falling, though it left no trace on the
damp road and pavements. Carbury
Street—at best a cheerless row of un-
homelike dwellings—had to Sacheverell's
overwrought mind a terribly ominous
gloom. In Number 14, one light was
burning on the second floor; he guessed
it was Anna's sitting-room. He walked
up the steps slowly—with no gladness,
no hope, only a weight at his heart.
A dull little maid-servant ushered him
up the stairs : he gave his name in a
voice he did not recognize ; the servant-

girl disappeared behind a *portière*, came out again and left him. As the door closed, the *portière* moved and Anna stood before him.

"Well?" she said, smiling, "well?"

Sacheverell put out his hand and just touched her. She was not a Spirit. She wore the dress he had last seen her in —one he knew well—a black garment of very ordinary make, threadbare but exquisitely neat. Her eyes were large, and shone with unearthly brightness: her face had a white radiance which was neither deathlike nor human. The beauty of her countenance made him dumb: he felt she had seen a glory he knew not of—nor guessed. She led him into an inner room—a tiny room lit by a flaring oil-lamp, badly trimmed and smelling of paraffin. Again they faced each other.

"I cannot see you very well," said

Anna, at last, "but you are the same—
a little thinner—but the same. Is it the
light on your hair or—is it grey? How
I wish I could see you better. I have
lived for this."

"Am I granite?" wondered Sacheverell, "am I human?" But he said
nothing.

"Tell me about *you*," said Anna;
"tell me about your Palace. Have you
a nice, big study—with a large window
and long shelves for your books? Does
it open on to the garden?"

"Oh, my dearest," said Sacheverell,
"have you been well taken care of?
Have you everything you wish? I want
to know—and I don't seem able——"

She laughed, and took his hand. "I
thought it was all ended twice. George
was very frightened—he soon loses his
nerve—but, you see, I am here." She
bent over him, and he thought she

kissed his forehead. "When can we have one of our old walks together? I cannot go far yet. Not more than two miles——"

"Two miles! My dearest——"

"Don't you believe me? I can—I am sure I could—with you."

"No," he stammered, "no—not yet. The weather—the weather is not bright enough. You must rest a little longer. Perhaps in March."

Her eyes looked far away: she seemed a little disappointed. "In March," she repeated; "but it is only February, now. In March!"

"Anna," he said, "I have known — I have always known — when you were suffering. Where is Christian? Does he take care of you?"

"He thinks he is being very kind," she said; "he means to be, at any rate."

"I will forgive him everything," said

Sacheverell, "if he takes care of you."

"Don't you see," she said, "don't you understand—that *his* care is what is killing me? That it *has* killed me? I feel as though I were in prison. I cannot tell him so. I cannot tell the doctors so. Besides, I am too weak to be moved. Mine was the mistake. I should not have returned to him. But I could not let him die. The very sight of him," she said again, "kills me."

"I know—I know, I *knew*," he said.

"Don't let us talk of it. In March—perhaps something will happen in March. You said March, didn't you? I am supposed to be suffering from a sort of over-work. I shall never finish 'Pompilia' now. But tell me about *you*."

"How are your money matters?" he said, abruptly. The question was wrung from him. He looked round the shabby, cold room, and hated himself and his palace.

"In a few weeks I shall be in the poorhouse," said Anna, laughing. "A new experience! It will all be useful to my work. Local colour!"

"Anna," he said, desperately, "you *must* let me——"

"I am only in fun, of course," she said. "If I wanted anything, I would tell you. You know I would. But I shall soon be well again, and away from here. If only my eyes—— Let me look at you once more." She sighed at last, and turned away. He saw a tear roll down her cheek. "Do you think," she said, "we shall ever see the Studio—again?"

He made no answer, but, following a blind instinct, caught her hand. He knew afterwards that it was a pitiful effort to hold her from Death.

"I suppose you must go now," she said. He felt that this was her way of telling him that her strength was failing. He rose, and kissed her good-bye. "I *have* lived, dearest," said Anna.

A little later he found himself in the street. All feeling had left him : he had no mind—not even enough to wonder whether his soul were dead. He walked into the gathering darkness—on and on. Then by degrees he remembered that the meeting he had longed, without hoping for—had taken place. He had gained his heart's desire : he had seen Anna once more—spoken to her— touched her—heard her voice. Swifter than words the thought rushed over him that he must see her again and explain : he had been cold, distant, speechless, impossible.

He drove back to Carbury Street.

The landlady opened the door this

time.   She told him that Mrs. Christian
was resting on the sofa : she had not
felt quite strong enough yet to go up-
stairs to her room.   She was wonderful
easy tired.   But she would, no doubt,
see him.

"I was obliged to come back, Anna,"
he said, when he saw her.   "I think my
heart is broken ; but, you know—I love
you.   Words are nothing."

Anna laughed.   "I understand, of
course," she said.   "How could I misunderstand you ?   My dearest and best
—my very dearest."

He drew a long sigh.   "If you understand," he said, "that is enough.   But I
wanted to make sure."   He knelt down
by her side, and kissed her hands.

"It is not every one," she said, "who
can say—as I can say—I have found
perfect happiness and perfect love.   I
think of that, and forget everything

else. Good-bye. You will come again
—soon ? "

" Soon," he said.

In the hall he met a man, drunken,
not ill-featured, but of evil expression.
He reeled past Sacheverell with a dull
stare, and groped his way up the stair-
case, bawling :—

"It is not mine to sing the stately grace,
The sweet soul shining in my lady's face.
Not mine in glo-glorious melodies—"

It was George Christian. And it was
for him to close her eyes in death.

XI.

Two days later, Sacheverell received a letter from Mrs. Grimmage.

"Sir,—Mrs. Christian died suddenly this morning. She sent for me, poor dear lady. I am too upset to write more. My lord, your obedient,

"E. Grimmage."

"Have you got bad news, Peter?" said Mrs. Molle. They were sitting at the luncheon-table. He had already told her of Anna's illness, and she had guessed the rest—or enough. As the woman was dying (by a Special Providence), she viewed the situation with complacency.   " Is it bad news? " she repeated.

" I expected it," he said, briefly, and left the room.

The blow had fallen : he could weep —a little.   The heart-breaking anxiety, the terrible despair of the past four months' vanished like evil spirits : he felt and believed that she was with him : that they were together as they had never been even when life seemed fairest.   And, as he looked into the Past, he saw how they both—by silent agreement — had left the End un-imagined.   With them each day had been but a Beginning.

And now it was Finished.

When Sacheverell entered the chamber of death he saw Anna lying on the bed, her hands folded on her breast, her eyes closed as though she were resting them.

Such beauty and such peace were beyond all words or tears. He knelt down by the bedside. . . .

He was next conscious of another presence in the room. He looked up, and saw Sir Richard Kilcoursie.

Kilcoursie was the first to speak. " I have just returned," he said, catching his breath, " from my honeymoon. . . . Some one called Grimmage sent me word. . . . I loved her," he added, fiercely, " I loved her. I never knew how much. Do you think she knows ? She looks so still. She was always out of my reach, and now—for ever. . . . I was never good enough. There was no one like her. No one."

Sacheverell bowed his head.

They heard the sound of sobbing behind them. It was Mrs. Grimmage.

" Doesn't she look beautiful ? " she said, wiping her eyes. " I have never seen nothing to equal it. . . . We did all we could. We might have saved her if she'd have given in sooner. But she never would give in. She kept on saying, ' I shall soon be all right again,' and she wouldn't have the doctor in till this last week or two. She worked herself to death—and starved, if the truth was known. It's my firm belief that she only had a dinner when I reg'lar sat down and made her. I don't believe in them lunches she used to *say* she had at the Studio. . . . And that husband of hers was always nagging for money, and she gave it till there was next to nothing left but bare rent. I have been putting two and two together, and that's my con-clusion. It's cruel hard, it is. She might ha' eat me out of house and home, poor dear, for less than the asking. It's a life thrown away, that's what it is. Clean thrown away. And that husband of hers, with his three changes of air a year and a hot lunch every day of his life—*he* flourishes, he does. He's up-stairs now—taking on. You never see'd such antics. Reg'lar high-strikes. He's fit to bust hisself crying. But he's got just enough sense to stop before the bust comes. Let him howl! That's what I say. Let him howl! . . . There ain't no use trying to understand Providence. To take *her* and leave *him !* "

" I could not wish her back," said Sacheverell. He bent over and kissed Anna's brow — marble-cold and more radiant than the lilies on her breast— and then passed out of the room. Her spirit followed him : he left Kilcoursie gazing at her dead body.

When he reached home it was late in the evening. But he sat down to work at his sermon for the following Sunday. And he worked well ; writing had not

been so easy to him for months—for
months it had been a painful labour.

Eleanor watched him curiously. His
calmness seemed to her a little unfeeling.
She had always given him credit for a
certain amount of heart. She could only
compare his position to her own when
the Major died, and she had been dis-
tracted. Her prostrate condition had
been the talk of every tea-party in
Ballincollig for weeks. If Peter *had*
been in love with that extraordinary
artist-woman, he certainly had a very
singular way of showing it.

"Will you preach to-morrow, as
usual?" she ventured to say.

"Of course," he said, without looking
up from his paper. "Shall I not live as
she would have me live—working?"

But the Future, as he saw it, was
dim. . . .

Some years afterwards the Bishop of

Gaunt confided his brief love-story to a friend.

"But why," said the friend, "since the husband had forfeited every right to be considered, why didn't you punch his head and bear the woman off in triumph?"

"To tell the truth," said Sacheverell, "I was tempted to some such decisive measure—sorely tempted."

"If you had succumbed," said the friend, drily, "she would have recovered."

"Don't say so," said Sacheverell, putting out his hand; "*I think I know it.*"

The friend, who was a psychologist, went home with more material for his great work on *Impulse and Reason.*

If the gods have no sense of humour they must weep a great deal.

The Gresham Press,

UNWIN BROTHERS,

CHILWORTH AND LONDON.

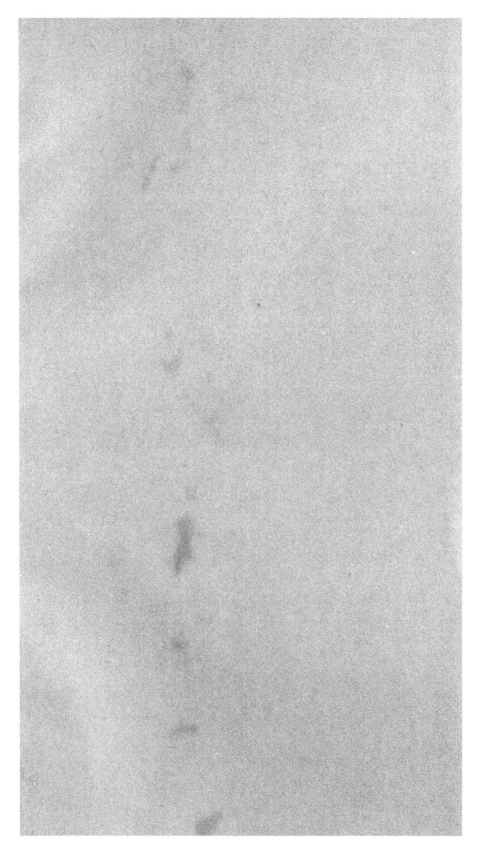

ImTheStory.com

Personalized Classic Books in many genre's

Unique gift for kids, partners, friends, colleagues

Customize:

- Character Names
- Upload your own front/back cover images (optional)
- Inscribe a personal message/dedication on the

    inside page (optional)

Customize many titles Including
- Alice in Wonderland
- Romeo and Juliet
- The Wizard of Oz
- A Christmas Carol
- Dracula
- Dr. Jekyll & Mr. Hyde
- And more...

Emily's Adventures in Wonderland

Ryan & Julia

CPSIA information can be obtained
at www.ICGtesting.com
Printed in the USA
BVHW070306290119
538842BV00031B/2169/P